PRESENTED TO

BY

Published by J. Countryman, a division of Thomas Nelson Inc.,
Nashville, Tennessee 37214

Compiled and edited by Terri Gibbs

Designed by Koechel Peterson and Associates, Inc.
Minneapolis, Minnesota

Illustrations © John S. Dykes / SIS

Illustrator John S. Dykes creates visual magic for corporate
and editorial giants including American Express, AT&T, *The
LA Times, The New York Times, Entertainment Weekly* and
Time Magazine. His unique ability to communicate on canvas
has won him numerous awards.

ISBN: 0-8499-5342-1

GOD'S ROADMAP
FOR NEW BEGINNINGS

Let the Journey Begin

MAX LUCADO

CONTENTS

Prologue—Teach Us to Pray

Preface

DEEP IN EVERY HEART
YOU WILL FIND IT: A LONGING
FOR MEANING, A QUEST FOR PURPOSE.

If you ask the secularists what is the meaning of life they will say, "We don't know." At best they might agree that we are developed animals. At worst, rearranged space dust.

What a contrast to God's vision for life: "We are God's handiwork, created in Christ Jesus to devote ourselves to the good deeds for which God has designed us" (Eph. 2:10 NEB).

God has placed his hand on your shoulder and said, "You're something special."

Untethered by time, he sees us all. In fact, he saw us before we were born.

And he loves what he sees. Flooded by emotion. Overcome by pride, the Starmaker turns to us, one by one, and says, "You are my child. I love you dearly."

And he loves us forever. Should you ever turn from him and walk away, he has already provided a way back. Nothing can separate you from his love. If you anchor these truths firmly in your heart, you will be ready for whatever you may encounter on the road ahead.

So let the journey begin!

Max Lucado
January 1998

What a God!

Ponder the achievement of God.

He doesn't condone our sin, nor does he compromise his standard.

He doesn't ignore our rebellion, nor does he relax his demands.

Rather than dismiss our sin, he assumes our sin and, incredibly, sentences himself.

God's holiness is honored. Our sin is punished . . . and we are redeemed.

God does what we cannot do so we can be what we dare not dream: perfect before God.

In the Grip of Grace

God's Plan for the Journey of Life— A Roadmap for Success

The key question in life is not
"How strong am I?" but rather
"How strong is God?"

Direction for the Road Ahead

OCCUPY YOURSELF WITH THE
NATURE OF GOD, NOT THE SIZE
OF YOUR BICEPS. . . .

That's what God told Moses to do. Remember the conversation at the burning bush? The tone was set in the first sentence. "Take off your sandals because you are standing on holy ground" (Exodus 3:5). With these eleven words Moses is enrolled in a class on God. Immediately the roles are defined. God is holy. Approaching him on even a quarter-inch of leather is too pompous. . . . No time is spent convincing Moses what Moses can do, but much time is spent explaining to Moses what God can do.

You and I tend to do the opposite. We would explain to Moses how he is ideally suited to return to Egypt. . . . Then we'd remind Moses how perfect he is for wilderness travel. . . . We'd spend time reviewing with Moses his resume and strengths.

But God doesn't. The strength of Moses is never considered. No pep talk is given, no pats on the backs are offered. Not one word is spoken to recruit Moses. But many words are used to reveal God. The strength of Moses is not the issue; the strength of God is.

The Great House of God

3

Nails didn't hold God to a cross.
Love did.

The Strength of God's Love

"Can anything make me stop loving you?" God asks. "Watch me speak your language, sleep on your earth, and feel your hurts. Behold the maker of sight and sound as he sneezes, coughs, and blows his nose. You wonder if I understand how you feel? Look into the dancing eyes of the kid in Nazareth; that's God walking to school. Ponder the toddler at Mary's table; that's God spilling his milk.

"You wonder how long my love will last? Find your answer on a splintered cross, on a craggy hill. That's me you see up there, your maker, your God, nail-stabbed and bleeding. Covered in spit and sin-soaked. That's your sin I'm feeling. That's your death I'm dying. That's your resurrection I'm living. That's how much I love you."

In the Grip of Grace

*You change your life
by changing your heart.*

Locked Behind Bars

Think of it this way. Sin put you in prison. Sin locked you behind the bars of guilt and shame and deception and fear. Sin did nothing but shackle you to the wall of misery. Then Jesus came and paid your bail. He served your time; he satisfied the penalty and set you free. Christ died, and when you cast your lot with him, your old self died too.

The only way to be set free from the prison of sin is to serve its penalty. In this case the penalty is death. Someone has to die, either you or a heaven-sent substitute. You cannot leave prison unless there is a death. But that death has occurred at Calvary. And when Jesus died, you died to sin's claim on your life. You are free.

In the Grip of Grace

Though we were spiritually dead because of the things we did against God, he gave us new life with Christ (Eph. 2:5).

A New Player on Our Team

As youngsters, we neighborhood kids would play street football. The minute we got home from school, we'd drop the books and hit the pavement. The kid across the street had a dad with a great and a strong addiction to football. As soon as he'd pull in the driveway from work we'd start yelling for him to come and play ball. He couldn't resist. Out of fairness he'd always ask, "Which team is losing?" Then he would join that team, which often seemed to be mine.

His appearance in the huddle changed the whole ball game. He was confident, strong, and most of all, he had a plan. We'd circle around him, and he'd look at us and say, "OK boys, here is what we are going to do." The other side was groaning before we left the huddle. You see, we not only had a new plan, we had a new leader.

He brought new life to our team. God does precisely the same. We didn't need a new play; we needed a new plan. We didn't need to trade positions; we needed a new player. That player is Jesus Christ, God's firstborn son.

In the Grip of Grace

STOP

Answer the big question of eternity, and the little questions of life fall into perspective.

Truth Will Triumph

Imagine that you are an ice skater in competition. You are in first place with one more round to go. If you perform well, the trophy is yours. You are nervous, anxious, and frightened.

Then, only minutes before your performance, your trainer rushes to you with the thrilling news: "You've already won! The judges tabulated the scores, and the person in second place can't catch you. You are too far ahead."

Upon hearing that news, how will you feel? Exhilarated!

And how will you skate? Timidly? Cautiously? Of course not. How about courageously and confidently? You bet you will. You will do your best because the prize is yours. You will skate like a champion because that is what you are! You will hear the applause of victory. . . .

The point is clear: the truth will triumph. The Father of truth will win, and the followers of truth will be saved.

The Applause of Heaven

*Faith is the grit in the soul
that puts the dare into dreams.*

Character Creates Courage

A legend from India tells about a mouse who was terrified of cats until a magician agreed to transform him into a cat. That resolved his fear . . . until he met a dog, so the magician changed him into a dog. The mouse-turned-cat-turned-dog was content until he met a tiger—so, once again, the magician changed him into what he feared. But when the tiger came complaining that he had met a hunter, the magician refused to help. "I will make you into a mouse again, for though you have the body of a tiger, you still have the heart of a mouse."

Sound familiar? How many people do you know who have built a formidable exterior, only to tremble inside with fear? We tackle our anxieties by taking on the appearance of a tiger. We face our fears with force. . . .

Or if we don't use force, we try other methods. We stockpile wealth. We seek security in things. We cultivate fame and seek status.

But do these approaches work? Can power, possessions, or popularity really deliver us from our fears? . . .

Courage is an outgrowth of who we are. Exterior supports may temporarily sustain, but only inward character creates courage.

The Applause of Heaven

God would prefer we have an occasional limp than a perpetual strut. And if it takes a thorn for him to make his point, he loves us enough not to pluck it out.

When God Says No

THERE ARE TIMES WHEN
THE ONE THING YOU WANT IS THE
ONE THING YOU NEVER GET. . . .

All you want is an open door or an extra day or an answered prayer, for which you will be thankful.

And so you pray and wait.

No answer.

You pray and wait.

No answer.

You pray and wait.

May I ask a very important question? What if God says no?

What if the request is delayed or even denied? When God says no to you, how will you respond? If God says, "I've given you my grace, and that is enough," will you be content?

Content. That's the word. A state of heart in which you would be at peace if God gave you nothing more than he already has. Test yourself with this question: What if God's only gift to you were his grace to save you. Would you be content? . . .

What if his answer is, "My grace is enough." Would you be content?

You see, from heaven's perspective, grace is enough.

In the Grip of Grace

If you want to touch God's heart,
use the name he loves to hear.
Call him Father.

We All Need a Father

[Recently], my daughter Jenna and I spent several days in the old city of Jerusalem. . . . One afternoon, as we were exiting the Jaffa gate, we found ourselves behind an orthodox Jewish family—a father and his three small girls. One of the daughters, perhaps four or five years of age, fell a few steps behind and couldn't see her father. *"Abba!"* she called to him. He stopped and looked. Only then did he realize he was separated from his daughter. *"Abba!"* she called again. He spotted her and immediately extended his hand. . . .

He held her hand tightly in his as they descended the ramp. . . . When the signal changed, he led her and her sisters through the intersection. In the middle of the street, he reached down and swung her up into his arms and continued their journey.

Isn't that what we all need? An *abba* who will hear when we call? Who will take our hand when we are weak? Who will guide us through the hectic intersections of life? Don't we all need an *abba* who will swing us up into his arms and carry us home? We all need a father.

The Great House of God

Even Jesus was given a portion
he found hard to swallow. But with God's
help, he did (Matt. 26:39).

Not Every Day Is a Three-Cookie Day

Last night during family devotions, I called my daughters to the table and set a plate in front of each. In the center of the table I placed a collection of food: some fruit, some raw vegetables, and some Oreo cookies. "Every day," I explained, "God prepares for us a plate of experiences. What kind of plate do you most enjoy?"

The answer was easy. Sara put three cookies on her plate. Some days are like that, aren't they? Some days are "three-cookie days." Many are not. Sometimes our plate has nothing but vegetables—twenty-four hours of celery, carrots, and squash. Apparently God knows we need some strength, and though the portion may be hard to swallow, isn't it for our own good? Most days, however, have a bit of it all. Vegetables, which are healthy but dull. Fruit, which tastes better and we enjoy. And even an Oreo, which does little for our nutrition, but a lot for our attitude. . . .

The next time your plate has more broccoli than apple pie, remember who prepared the meal. And the next time your plate has a portion you find hard to swallow, talk to God about it. Jesus did.

The Great House of God

*Don't ask God
to do what
you want.
Ask God to do
what is right.*

The Cure for Disappointment

WHEN GOD DOESN'T DO WHAT WE
WANT, IT'S NOT EASY. NEVER HAS BEEN.
NEVER WILL BE. BUT FAITH IS THE
CONVICTION THAT GOD KNOWS MORE
THAN WE DO ABOUT THIS LIFE AND HE
WILL GET US THROUGH IT.

Remember, disappointment is cured by revamped expectations.

I like the story about the fellow who went to the pet store in search of a singing parakeet. Seems he was a bachelor and his house was too quiet. The store owner had just the bird for him, so the man bought it.

The next day the bachelor came home from work to a house full of music. He went to the cage to feed the bird and noticed for the first time that the parakeet had only one leg.

He felt cheated that he'd been sold a one-legged bird, so he called and complained.

"What do you want," the store owner responded, "a bird who can sing or a bird who can dance?"

Good question for times of disappointment.

"How to Study the Bible"

God's gladness is not received by those
who earn it, but by those who admit they
don't deserve it.

God Promises Gladness

Nine times he promises it. And he promises it to an unlikely crowd:

- *"The poor in spirit."* Beggars in God's soup kitchen.

- *"Those who mourn."* Sinners Anonymous bound together by the truth of their introduction: "Hi, I am me. I'm a sinner."

- *"The meek."* Pawnshop pianos played by Van Cliburn. (He's so good no one notices the missing keys.)

- *"Those who hunger and thirst."* Famished orphans who know the difference between a TV dinner and a Thanksgiving feast.

- *"The merciful."* Winners of the million-dollar lottery who share the prize with their enemies.

- *"The pure in heart."* Physicians who love lepers and escape infection.

- *"The peacemakers."* Architects who build bridges with wood from a Roman cross.

- *"The persecuted."* Those who manage to keep an eye on heaven while walking through hell on earth.

It is to this band of pilgrims that God promises a special blessing. A heavenly joy. A sacred delight.

But this joy is not cheap. What Jesus promises is not a gimmick to give you goose bumps nor a mental attitude that has to be pumped up at pep rallies. No, Matthew 5 describes God's radical reconstruction of the heart.

The Applause of Heaven

Have You Lost Your Hearing?

Once there was a man who dared God to speak.
Burn the bush like you did for Moses, God.
And I will follow.
Collapse the walls like you did for Joshua, God.
And I will fight.
Still the waves like you did on Galilee, God.
And I will listen.
And so the man sat by a bush, near a wall, close to the sea
and waited for God to speak.

And God heard the man, so God answered.
He sent fire, not for a bush, but for a church.
He brought down a wall, not of brick, but of sin.
He stilled a storm, not of the sea, but of a soul.

And God waited for the man to respond.
And he waited . . .
And he waited . . .
And waited.

But because the man was looking at bushes, not hearts; bricks and not lives, seas and not souls, he decided that God had done nothing.
Finally he looked to God and asked, *Have you lost your power?*
And God looked at him and said, *Have you lost your hearing?*

A Gentle Thunder

Stop, Look, and Listen—
Good Habits for a Good Journey

*Growth is the goal of the Christian.
Maturity is mandatory.*

Healthy Habits

I like the story of the little boy who fell out of bed. When his Mom asked him what happened, he answered, "I don't know. I guess I stayed too close to where I got in."

Easy to do the same with our faith. It's tempting just to stay where we got in and never move.

Pick a time in the not-too-distant past. A year or two ago. Now ask yourself a few questions. How does your prayer life today compare with then? How about your giving? Have both the amount and the joy increased? What about your church loyalty? Can you tell you've grown? And Bible study? Are you learning to learn? . . .

There they are. Four habits worth having. Isn't it good to know that some habits are good for you? Make them a part of your day and grow. Don't make the mistake of the little boy. Don't stay too close to where you got in. It's risky resting on the edge.

When God Whispers Your Name

STOP

Your prayer on earth activates God's power in heaven, and "God's will is done on earth as it is in heaven."

Prayers Are Precious Jewels

You can talk to God because God listens. Your voice matters in heaven. He takes you very seriously. When you enter his presence, the attendants turn to you to hear your voice. No need to fear that you will be ignored. Even if you stammer or stumble, even if what you have to say impresses no one, it impresses God—and he listens. . . .

Intently. Carefully. The prayers are honored as precious jewels. Purified and empowered, the words rise in a delightful fragrance to our Lord. . . . Your words do not stop until they reach the very throne of God. . . .

Your prayers move God to change the world. You may not understand the mystery of prayer. You don't need to. But this much is clear: Actions in heaven begin when someone prays on earth. What an amazing thought!

The Great House of God

The problem is not that God hasn't spoken but that we haven't listened.

Set Your Compass in the Right Direction

Imagine your reaction if I were to take a telephone book, open it up, and proclaim, *I have found a list of everyone who's on welfare!* Or what if I said, *Here is a list of college graduates!* Or, *This book will tell us who has a red car.* You'd probably say, "Now wait a minute—that's not the purpose of that book. You're holding a *telephone book.* Its purpose is simply to reveal the name and number of residents of a city during a certain time frame."

Only by understanding its purpose can I accurately use the telephone book. Only by understanding its purpose can I accurately use the Bible. . . .

The purpose of the Bible is simply to proclaim God's plan to save his children. It asserts that man is lost and needs to be saved. And it communicates the message that Jesus is the God in the flesh sent to save his children.

Though the Bible was written over sixteen centuries by at least forty authors, it has one central theme—salvation through faith in Christ. Begun by Moses in the lonely desert of Arabia and finished by John on the lonely Isle of Patmos, it is held together by a strong thread: God's passion and God's plan to save his children.

What a vital truth! Understanding the purpose of the Bible is like setting the compass in the right direction. Calibrate it correctly and you'll journey safely. But fail to set it, and who knows where you'll end up.

"How to Study the Bible"

Someone who sees grace as permission
to sin has missed grace entirely.
Mercy understood is holiness desired.

Grace Teaches Us How to Live

Do we ever compromise tonight, knowing we'll confess tomorrow?

It's easy to be like the fellow visiting Las Vegas who called the preacher, wanting to know the hours of the Sunday service. The preacher was impressed. "Most people who come to Las Vegas don't do so to go to church."

"Oh, I'm not coming for the church. I'm coming for the gambling and parties and wild women. If I have half as much fun as I intend to, I'll need a church come Sunday morning."

Is that the intent of grace? Is God's goal to promote disobedience? Hardly. "Grace . . . teaches us not to live against God nor to do the evil things the world wants us to do. Instead, that grace teaches us to live now in a wise and right way and in a way that shows we serve God" (Titus 2:11–12). God's grace has released us from selfishness. Why return?

In the Grip of Grace

STOP

You were made free from sin,
and now you are slaves to goodness
(Rom. 6:17–18).

Exposed to a Higher Standard

Most of my life I've been a closet slob. I was slow to see the logic of neatness. Why make up a bed if you are going to sleep in it again tonight? Does it make sense to wash dishes after only one meal? Isn't it easier to leave your clothes on the floor at the foot of the bed so they'll be there when you get up and put them on? . . .

Then I got married. . . .

I enrolled in a twelve-step program for slobs. ("My name is Max, I hate to vacuum.") A physical therapist helped me rediscover the muscles used for hanging shirts and placing toilet paper on the holder. My nose was reintroduced to the fragrance of Pine Sol. . . .

Then came the moment of truth. Denalyn went out ot town for a week. Initially I reverted to the old man. I figured I'd be a slob for six days and clean on the seventh. But something strange happened, a curious discomfort. I couldn't relax with dirty dishes in the sink.

What had happened to me?

Simple. I'd been exposed to a higher standard.

Isn't that what has happened with us? . . .

Before Christ our lives were out of control, sloppy, and indulgent. We didn't even know we were slobs until we met him. . . .

Suddenly we find ourselves wanting to do good. Go back to the old mess? Are you kidding?

In the Grip of Grace

Those who keep secrets from God keep their distance from God. Those who are honest with God draw near to God.

The Bridge of Confession

Once there were a couple of farmers who couldn't get along with each other. A wide ravine separated their two farms, but as a sign of their mutual distaste for each other, each constructed a fence on his side of the chasm to keep the other out.

In time, however, the daughter of one met the son of the other, and the couple fell in love. Determined not to be kept apart by the folly of their fathers, they tore down the fence and used the wood to build a bridge across the ravine.

Confession does that. Confessed sin becomes the bridge over which we can walk back into the presence of God.

In the Grip of Grace

STOP

God loves my neighbor
and makes him my brother.

Rocking the Boat

God has enlisted us in his navy and placed us on his ship. The boat has one purpose—to carry us safely to the other shore.

This is no cruise ship; it's a battleship. We aren't called to a life of leisure; we are called to a life of service. Each of us has a different task. Some, concerned with those who are drowning, are snatching people from the water. Others are occupied with the enemy, so they man the cannons of prayer and worship. Still others devote themselves to the crew, feeding and training the crew members.

Though different, we are the same. Each can tell of a personal encounter with the captain, for each has received a personal call. He found us among the shanties of the seaport and incited us to follow him. Our faith was born at the sight of his fondness, and so we went.

We each followed him across the gangplank of his grace onto the same boat. There is one captain and one destination. Though the battle is fierce, the boat is safe, for our captain is God. The ship will not sink. For that, there is no concern.

In the Grip of Grace

*In the grip of grace,
you're free to be honest.*

Honest to God

I MADE A MISTAKE IN HIGH SCHOOL. . . .

Our baseball coach had a firm rule against chewing tobacco. We had a couple of players who were known to sneak a chew, and he wanted to call it to our attention.

He got our attention, all right. Before long we'd all tried it. A sure test of manhood was to take a chew when the pouch was passed down the bench. I had barely made the team; I sure wasn't going to fail the test of manhood.

One day I'd just popped a plug in my mouth when one of the players warned, "Here comes the coach!" Not wanting to get caught, I did what came naturally, I swallowed. *Gulp.*

I added new meaning to the scripture, "I felt weak deep inside me. I moaned all day long. . . . My strength was gone as in the summer heat." I paid the price for hiding my disobedience.

My body was not made to ingest tobacco. Your soul was not made to invest sin.

May I ask a frank question? Are you keeping any secrets from God? Any parts of your life off limits? Any cellars boarded up or attics locked? Any part of your past or present that you hope you and God never discuss? . . .

Take a pointer from a nauseated third baseman. You'll feel better if you get it out.

In the Grip of Grace

*We discover gladness when
we leave the prison of pride and
repent of our rebellion.*

The Soil of the Soul

Confession does for the soul what preparing the land does for the field. Before the farmer sows the seed he works the acreage, removing the rocks and pulling the stumps. He knows that seed grows better if the land is prepared. Confession is the act of inviting God to walk the acreage of our hearts. "There is a rock of greed over here Father, I can't budge it. And that tree of guilt near the fence? Its roots are long and deep. And may I show you some dry soil, too crusty for seed?" God's seed grows better if the soil of the heart is cleared.

And so the Father and the Son walk the field together; digging and pulling, preparing the heart for fruit. Confession invites the Father to work the soil of the soul.

Confession seeks pardon from God, not amnesty. Pardon presumes guilt; amnesty, derived from the same Greek word as *amnesia*, "forgets" the alleged offense without imputing guilt. Confession admits wrong and seeks forgiveness; amnesty denies wrong and claims innocence.

In the Grip of Grace

Which Will Be Your Choice?

On one side stands the crowd.
Jeering.
Baiting.
Demanding.

On the other stands a peasant.
Swollen lips.
Lumpy eye.
Lofty promise.

One promises acceptance,
the other a cross.
One offers flesh and flash,
the other offers faith.

The crowd challenges, "Follow us and fit in."
Jesus promises, "Follow me and stand out."

They promise to please.
God promises to save. . . .

God looks at you and asks . . .
Which will be your choice?

A Gentle Thunder

A Fork in the Road—
Deciding Which Way to Go

Claiming themselves to be wise without God, they became utter fools instead (Rom. 1:22 TLB).

The Purpose of Life

MINE DEEP ENOUGH IN EVERY
HEART AND YOU'LL FIND IT:
A LONGING FOR MEANING,
A QUEST FOR PURPOSE. AS SURELY
AS A CHILD BREATHES, HE WILL
SOMEDAY WONDER, "WHAT IS THE
PURPOSE OF MY LIFE?"

Some search for meaning in a career. "My purpose is to be a dentist." Fine vocation but hardly a justification for existence. They opt to be a human "doing" rather than a human "being." Who they are is what they do; consequently they do a lot. They work many hours because if they don't work, they don't have an identity.

For others, who they are is what they have. They find meaning in a new car or a new house or new clothes. These people are great for the economy and rough on the budget because they are always seeking meaning in something they own. . . .

Some try sports, entertainment, cults, sex, you name it.

All mirages in the desert of purpose. . . .

Shouldn't we face the truth? If we don't acknowledge God, we are flotsam in the universe.

In the Grip of Grace

God is not the God of confusion, and wherever he sees sincere seekers with confused hearts, you can bet your sweet December that he will do whatever it takes to help them see his will.

Knowing God's Will

We learn God's will by spending time in his presence. The key to knowing God's heart is having a relationship with him. A *personal* relationship. God will speak to you differently than he will speak to others. Just because God spoke to Moses through a burning bush, that doesn't mean we should all sit next to a bush waiting for God to speak. God used a fish to convict Jonah. Does that mean we should have worship services at Sea World? No. God reveals his heart personally to each person.

For that reason, your walk with God is essential. His heart is not seen in an occasional chat or weekly visit. We learn his will as we take up residence in his house every single day. . . .

Walk with him long enough and you come to know his heart.

The Great House of God

I Choose Love

It's quiet. It's early. My coffee is hot. The sky is still black. The world is still asleep. The day is coming.

In a few moments the day will arrive. It will roar down the track with the rising of the sun. The stillness of the dawn will be exchanged for the noise of the day. The calm of solitude will be replaced by the pounding pace of the human race. The refuge of the early morning will be invaded by decisions to be made and deadlines to be met.

For the next twelve hours I will be exposed to the day's demands. It is now that I must make a choice. Because of Calvary, I'm free to choose. And so I choose.

I choose love . . .

No occasion justifies hatred; no injustice warrants bitterness. I choose love. Today I will love God and what God loves.

I choose joy . . .

I will invite my God to be the God of circumstance. I will refuse the temptation to be cynical . . . the tool of the lazy thinker. I will refuse to see people as anything less than human beings, created by God. I will refuse to see any problem as anything less than an opportunity to see God.

I choose peace . . .

I will live forgiven. I will forgive so that I may live.

I choose patience . . .

I will overlook the inconveniences of the world. Instead of cursing the one who takes my place, I'll invite him to do so. Rather than complain that the wait is too long, I will thank God for a moment to pray. Instead of clinching my fist at new assignments, I will face them with joy and courage.

I choose kindness . . .

I will be kind to the poor, for they are alone. Kind to the rich, for they are afraid. And kind to the unkind, for such is how God has treated me.

I choose goodness . . .

I will go without a dollar before I take a dishonest one. I will be overlooked before I will boast. I will confess before I will accuse. I choose goodness.

I choose faithfulness . . .

Today I will keep my promises. My debtors will not regret their trust. My associates will not question my word. My wife will not question my love. And my children will never fear that their father will not come home.

I choose gentleness . . .

Nothing is won by force. I choose to be gentle. If I raise my voice may it be only in praise. If I clench my fist, may it be only in prayer. If I make a demand, may it be only of myself.

I choose self-control . . .

I am a spiritual being. After this body is dead, my spirit will soar. I refuse to let what will rot, rule the eternal. I choose self-control. I will be drunk only by joy. I will be impassioned only by my faith. I will be influenced only by God. I will be taught only by Christ. I choose self-control.

Love, joy, peace, patience, kindness, goodness, faithfulness, gentleness, and self-control. To these I commit my day. If I succeed, I will give thanks. If I fail, I will seek his grace. And then, when this day is done, I will place my head on my pillow and rest.

STOP

*The fire of
your heart
is the light
of your path.*

The Fire of Your Heart

Want to know God's will for your life? Then answer this question: What ignites your heart? Forgotten orphans? Untouched nations? The inner city? The outer limits?

Heed the fire within!

Do you have a passion to sing? Then sing!

Are you stirred to manage? Then manage!

Do you ache for the ill? Then treat them!

Do you hurt for the lost? Then teach them!

As a young man I felt the call to preach. Unsure if I was correct in my reading of God's will for me, I sought the counsel of a minister I admired. His counsel still rings true. "Don't preach," he said, "unless you have to."

As I pondered his words I found my answer: "I *have* to. If I don't, the fire will consume me."

What is the fire that consumes you?

The Great House of God

Succeed in what matters.

A Passion for Excellence

The push for power has come to shove. And most of us are either pushing or being pushed.

I might point out the difference between a passion for excellence and a passion for power. The desire for excellence is a gift of God, much needed in society. It is characterized by respect for quality and a yearning to use God's gifts in a way that pleases him. . . .

There are certain things you can do that no one else can. Perhaps it is parenting, or constructing houses, or encouraging the discouraged. There are things that *only you* can do, and you are alive to do them. In the great orchestra we call life, you have an instrument and a song, and you owe it to God to play them both sublimely.

But there is a canyon of difference between doing your best to glorify God and doing whatever it takes to glorify yourself. The quest for excellence is a mark of maturity. The quest for power is childish.

The Applause of Heaven

STOP

No one is useless to God.
No one.

You Are One-of-a-Kind

In my closet hangs a sweater that I seldom wear. It is too small. The sleeves are too short, the shoulders too tight. Some of the buttons are missing, and the thread is frazzled. . . . Logic says I should clear out the space and get rid of the sweater.

That's what *logic* says.

But *love* won't let me.

Something unique about that sweater makes me keep it. What is unusual about it? . . .

It's the creation of a devoted mother expressing her love.

That sweater is unique. One of a kind. It can't be replaced. Each strand was chosen with care. Each thread was selected with affection.

And though the sweater has lost all of its use, it has lost none of its value. It is valuable not because of its function, but because of its maker.

That must have been what the psalmist had in mind when he wrote, "you knit me together in my mother's womb."

Think on those words. You were knitted together. You aren't an accident. You weren't mass-produced. You aren't an assembly-line product.

You were deliberately planned, specifically gifted, and lovingly positioned on this earth by the Master Craftsman. . . .

In a society that has little room for second fiddles, that's good news. . . . In a system that ranks the value of a human by the figures of his salary or the shape of her legs . . . let me tell you something: Jesus' plan is a reason for joy!

The Applause of Heaven

We are God's handiwork, created in Christ Jesus to devote ourselves to the good deeds for which God has designed us (Eph. 2:10 NEB).

God's Signature Makes You Special

With God in your world, you aren't an accident or an incident; you are a gift to the world, a divine work of art, signed by God.

One of the finest gifts I ever received is a football signed by thirty former professional quarterbacks. There is nothing unique about this ball. For all I know it was bought at a discount sports store. What makes it unique is the signatures.

The same is true with us. In the scheme of nature *Homo sapiens* are not unique. We aren't the only creatures with flesh and hair and blood and hearts. What makes us special is not only our body but the signature of God on our lives. We are his works of art. We are created in his image to do good deeds. We are significant, not because of what we do, but because of whose we are.

In the Grip of Grace

STOP

Just because you understand the system, that doesn't deny the presence of someone outside the system.

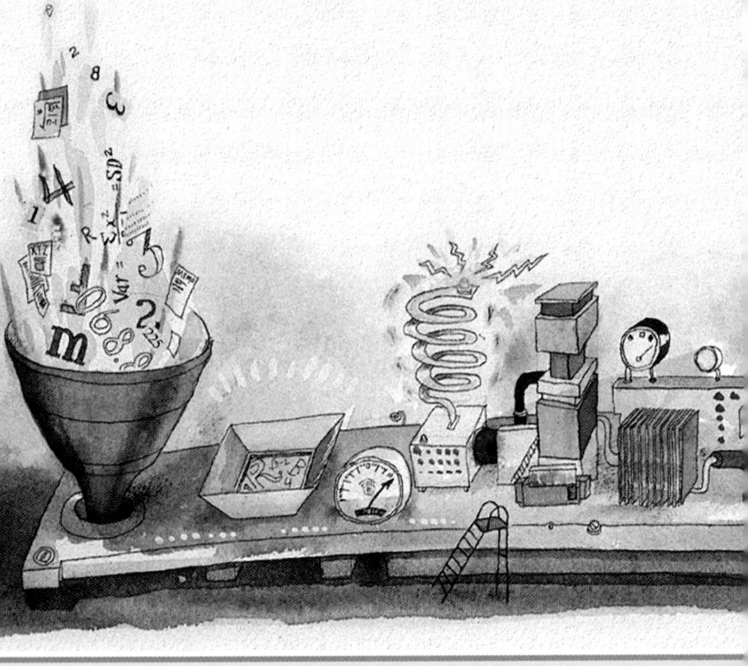

Got It All Figured Out

We understand how storms are created. We map solar systems and transplant hearts. We measure the depths of the oceans and send signals to distant planets. We . . . have studied the system and are learning how it works.

And, for some, the loss of mystery has led to the loss of majesty. The more we know, the less we believe. Strange, don't you think? Knowledge of the workings shouldn't negate wonder. Knowledge should stir wonder. Who has more reason to worship than the astronomer who has seen the stars? Than the surgeon who has held a heart? Than the oceanographer who has pondered the depths? The more we know, the more we should be amazed.

Ironically, the more we know, the less we worship. We are more impressed with our discovery of the light switch than with the one who invented electricity. . . . Rather than worship the Creator, we worship the creation (see Rom. 1:25).

No wonder there is no wonder. We've figured it all out.

In the Grip of Grace

STOP

The conclusion is unavoidable:
self-salvation simply does not work.

God's Highest Dream

Please note: Salvation is God-given, God-driven, God-empowered, and God-originated. The gift is not from man to God. It is from God to man. "It is not our love for God; it is God's love for us in sending his Son to be the way to take away our sins" (1 John 4:10). . . .

We have attempted to reach the moon but scarcely made it off the ground. We tried to swim the Atlantic, but couldn't get beyond the reef. We have attempted to scale the Everest of salvation, but we have yet to leave the base camp, much less ascend the slope. The quest is simply too great; we don't need more supplies or muscle or technique; we need a helicopter.

Can't you hear it hovering?

"God has a way to *make people right with him*" (Rom. 3:21, italics mine). How vital that we embrace this truth. God's highest dream is not to make us rich, not to make us successful or popular or famous. God's dream is to make us right with him.

In the Grip of Grace

Godlessness

The word defines itself. A life minus God.

Worse than a disdain for God, this is a disregard for God.

A disdain at least acknowledges his presence. Godlessness doesn't.

Whereas disdain will lead people to act with irreverance, disregard causes them to act as if God were irrelevant, as if he were not a factor in the journey.

In the Grip of Grace

Dangers and Detours Ahead—
Slow Down, Avoid Disaster

The right heart with the wrong creed is better than the right creed with the wrong heart.

Godless Living

Since the hedonist has never seen the hand who made the universe, he assumes there is no life beyond the here and now. He believes there is no truth beyond this room. No purpose beyond his own pleasure. No divine factor. He has no concern for the eternal. . . .

What happens when a culture settles for grass huts instead of the father's castle? Are there any consequences for a godless pursuit of pleasure? Is there a price to pay for living for today?

The hedonist says, "Who cares? I may be bad, but so what? What I do is my business." He's more concerned about satisfying his passions than in knowing the Father. His life is so desperate for pleasure that he has no time or room for God.

Is he right? Is it OK to spend our days thumbing our noses at God and living it up?

Paul says, "Absolutely not!"

According to Romans 1, we lose more than stained-glass windows when we dismiss God. We lose our standard, our purpose, and our worship. "Their thinking became useless. Their foolish minds were filled with darkness. They said they were wise, but they became fools" (Rom. 1:21–22).

In the Grip of Grace

STOP

You will never forgive anyone more than God has already forgiven you.

Revenge Is a Raging Fire

Resentment is the cocaine of the emotions. It causes our blood to pump and our enegy level to rise.

But, also like cocaine, it demands increasingly larger and more frequent dosages. There is a dangerous point at which anger ceases to be an emotion and becomes a driving force. A person bent on revenge moves unknowingly further and further away from being able to forgive, for to be without the anger is to be without a source of energy.

That explains why the bitter complain to anyone who will listen. They want—they need—to have their fire fanned. . . .

Resentment is like cocaine in another way, too. Cocaine can kill the addict. And anger can kill the angry. . . .

And it can be spiritually fatal, too. It shrivels the soul.

Hatred is the rabid dog that turns on its owner. Revenge is the raging fire that consumes the arsonist. Bitterness is the trap that snares the hunter.

And mercy is the choice that can set them all free.

The Applause of Heaven

God forgets the past. Imitate him.

Do You Have a Hole in Your Heart?

PERHAPS THE WOUND IS OLD. A PARENT ABUSED YOU. A TEACHER SLIGHTED YOU. . . .

And you are angry.

Or perhaps the wound is fresh. The friend who owes you money just drove by in a new car. The boss who hired you with promises of promotions has forgotten how to pronounce your name. Your circle of friends escaped on a weekend getaway, and you weren't invited. . . .

And you are hurt.

Part of you is broken, and the other part is bitter. Part of you wants to cry, and part of you wants to fight. The tears you cry are hot because they come from your heart, and there is a fire burning in your heart. It's the fire of anger. It's blazing. It's consuming. Its flames leap up under a steaming pot of revenge.

And you are left with a decision. "Do I put the fire out or heat it up? Do I get over it or get even? Do I release it or resent it? Do I let my hurts heal, or do I let hurt turn into hate?". . .

Resentment is the deliberate decision to nurse the offense until it becomes a black, furry, growling grudge. . . .

Unfaithfulness is wrong. Revenge is bad. But the worst part of all is that, without forgiveness, bitterness is all that is left.

The Applause of Heaven

*Conflict is inevitable,
but combat is optional.*

The Answer to Arguments

SOMETIME AGO MY WIFE BOUGHT
A MONKEY. I DIDN'T WANT A MONKEY
IN OUR HOUSE, SO I OBJECTED.

"Where is he going to eat?" I asked.
"At our table."
"Where is he going to sleep?" I inquired.
"In our bed."
"What about the odor?" I demanded.
"I got used to you; I guess the monkey can too."

Unity doesn't begin in examining others but in examining self. Unity begins not in demanding that others change, but in admitting that we aren't so perfect ourselves. . . .

The answer to arguments? Acceptance. The first step to unity? Acceptance. Not agreement, acceptance. Not unanimity, acceptance. Not negotiation, arbitration, or elaboration. Those might come later but only after the first step, acceptance.

In the Grip of Grace

*The more we immerse ourselves
in grace, the more likely we
are to give grace.*

Hatred Will Break Your Back

Oh, the gradual grasp of hatred. Its damage begins like the crack in my windshield. Thanks to a speeding truck on a gravel road, my window was chipped. With time the nick became a crack, and the crack became a winding tributary. Soon the windshield was a spider web of fragments. I couldn't drive my car without thinking of the jerk who drove too fast. Though I've never seen him, I could describe him. He is some deadbeat bum who cheats on his wife, drives with a six-pack on the seat, and keeps the television so loud the neighbors can't sleep. His carelessness blocked my vision. (Didn't do much for my view out the windshield either.)

Ever heard the expression "blind rage"?

Let me be very clear. Hatred will sour your outlook and break your back. The load of bitterness is simply too heavy. Your knees will buckle under the strain, and your heart will break beneath the weight. The mountain before you is steep enough without the heaviness of hatred on your back. The wisest choice— the *only* choice—is for you to drop the anger. You will never be called upon to give anyone more grace than God has already given you.

In the Grip of Grace

*Settling the score is done
at great expense.*

The High Cost of Getting Even

Have you ever noticed in the western movies how the bounty hunter travels alone? It's not hard to see why. Who wants to hang out with a guy who settles scores for a living? Who wants to risk getting on his bad side? More than once I've heard a person spew his anger. He thought I was listening, when really I was thinking, *I hope I never get on his list.* Cantankerous sorts, these bounty hunters. Best leave them alone. Hang out with the angry and you might catch a stray bullet. Debt-settling is a lonely occupation. It's also an unhealthy occupation. . . .

If you're out to settle the score, you'll never rest. How can you? For one thing, your enemy may never pay up. As much as you think you deserve an apology, your debtor may not agree. The racist may never repent. The chauvinist may never change. As justified as you are in your quest for vengeance, you may never get a penny's worth of justice. And if you do, will it be enough?

The Great House of God

*A stammering shepherd
in this generation may be the
mighty Moses of the next.*

Get Out of the Judgment Seat

We condemn a man for stumbling this morning, but we didn't see the blows he took yesterday. We judge a woman for the limp in her walk, but cannot see the tack in her shoe. We mock the fear in their eyes, but have no idea how many stones they have ducked or darts they have dodged.

Are they too loud? Perhaps they fear being neglected again. Are they too timid? Perhaps they fear failing again. Too slow? Perhaps they fell the last time they hurried. You don't know. Only one who has followed yesterday's steps can be their judge.

Not only are we ignorant about yesterday, we are ignorant about tomorrow. Dare we judge a book while chapters are yet unwritten? Should we pass a verdict on a painting while the artist still holds the brush? How can you dismiss a soul until God's work is complete? "God began doing a good work in you, and I am sure he will continue it until it is finished when Jesus Christ comes again" (Phil. 1:6).

In the Grip of Grace

God's delight is received upon surrender,
not awarded upon conquest.

Mountains You Weren't Made to Climb

THERE ARE CERTAIN MOUNTAINS
ONLY GOD CAN CLIMB. . . .

It's not that you aren't welcome to try, it's just that you aren't able. . . .

If the word *Savior* is in your job description, it's because you put it there. Your role is to help the world, not save it. Mount Messiah is one mountain you weren't made to climb.

Nor is Mount Self-Sufficient. You aren't able to run the world, nor are you able to sustain it. Some of you think you can. You are self-made. You don't bow your knees, you just roll up your sleeves and put in another twelve-hour day . . . which may be enough when it comes to making a living or building a business. But when you face your own grave or your own guilt, your power will not do the trick.

You were not made to run a kingdom, nor are you expected to be all-powerful. And you certainly can't handle all the glory. Mount Applause is the most seductive of the three peaks. The higher you climb the more people applaud, but the thinner the air becomes. More than one person has stood at the top and shouted, "Mine is the glory!" only to lose their balance and fall.

The Great House of God

The wages of sin is death . . .
(Rom. 6:23 NIV).

The Soul Killer

SIN IS A FATAL DISEASE.

Sin has sentenced us to a slow, painful death.

Sin does to a life what shears do to a flower. A cut at the stem separates a flower from the source of life. Initially the flower is attractive, still colorful and strong. But watch that flower over a period of time, and the leaves will wilt and the petals will drop. No matter what you do, the flower will never live again. Surround it with water. Stick the stem in soil. Baptize it with fertilizer. Glue the flower back on the stem. Do what you wish. The flower is dead. . . .

A dead soul has no life.

Cut off from God, the soul withers and dies. The consequence of sin is not a bad day or a bad mood but a dead soul. The sign of a dead soul is clear: poisoned lips and cursing mouths, feet that lead to violence and eyes that don't see God.

Now you know how people can be so vulgar. Their souls are dead. Now you see how some religions can be so oppressive. They have no life. Now you understand how the drug peddler can sleep at night and the dictator can live with his conscience. He has none.

The finished work of sin is to kill the soul.

In the Grip of Grace

STOP

God is angry at the evil that ruins his children.

God's Anger

GOD IS ANGRY AT EVIL.

For many, this is a revelation. Some assume God is a harried high-school principal, too busy monitoring the planets to notice us.

He's not.

Others assume he is a doting parent, blind to the evil of his children.

Wrong.

Still others insist he loves us so much he cannot be angry at our evil.

They don't understand that love is *always* angry at evil.

Many don't understand God's anger because they confuse the wrath of God with the wrath of man. The two have little in common. Human anger is typically self-driven and prone to explosions of temper and violent deeds. We get ticked off because we've been overlooked, neglected, or cheated. This is the anger of man. It is not, however, the anger of God.

God doesn't get angry because he doesn't get his way. He gets angry because disobedience always results in self-destruction. What kind of father sits by and watches his child hurt himself?

In the Grip of Grace

STOP

*Seems that God is looking more
for ways to get us home than for
ways to keep us out.*

Grace Isn't Logical

God's judgment has never been a problem for me. In fact, it always seemed right. Lightning bolts on Sodom. Fire on Gomorrah. *Good job, God.* Egyptians swallowed in the Red Sea. *They had it coming. . . .*

Discipline is easy for me to swallow. Logical to assimilate. Manageable and appropriate.

But God's grace? Anything but.

Examples? How much time do you have?

David the psalmist becomes David the voyeur, but by God's grace becomes David the psalmist again. . . .

The thief on the cross: hellbent and hung-out-to-die one minute, heaven-bound and smiling the next.

Story after story. Prayer after prayer. Surprise after surprise. . . .

I challenge you to find one soul who came to God seeking grace and did not find it. . . . Find one person who came seeking a second chance and left with a stern lecture.

I dare you. Search.

You won't find it.

When God Whispers Your Name

Praise to God

You are a great God.
Your character is holy.
Your truth is absolute.
Your strength is unending.
Your discipline is fair.

You are a great God.
The mountain of your knowledge has no peak.
The ocean of your love has no shore.
The fabric of your fidelity has no tear.
The rock of your word has no crack.

You are a great God.
Your patience surprises us.
Your beauty stuns us.
Your love stirs us.

You are a great God.
Your provisions are abundant for our needs.
Your light is adequate for our path.
Your grace is sufficient for our sins.

You are a great God.
We even declare with reluctant words, your plan
  is perfect.
You are never early, never late.
Never tardy, never quick.
You sent your Son in the fullness of time
  and will return at the consummation of time.
Your plan is perfect.
Bewildering. Puzzling. Troubling.
But perfect. . . .

From "He Reminded Us of You"
(A Prayer for a Friend)

Two Is Fine Company—
A Friend for the Journey

*We treat others as we perceive
God is treating us.*

God Is In Your Corner

When I was seven years old, I ran away from home. I'd had enough of my father's rules and decided I could make it on my own, thank you very much. With my clothes in a paper bag, I stormed out the back gate and marched down the alley. Like the prodigal son, I decided I needed no father. Unlike the prodigal son, I didn't go far. I got to the end of the alley and remembered I was hungry, so I went back home.

But though the rebellion was brief, it was rebellion nonetheless. And had you stopped me on that prodigal path between the fences and asked me who my father was, I just might have told you how I felt. I just might have said, "I don't need a father. I'm too big for the rules of my family. It's just me, myself and my paper bag.". . .

I didn't hear the rooster crow like Peter did. I didn't feel the fish belch like Jonah did. I didn't get a robe and a ring and sandals like the prodigal did. But I learned from my father on earth what those three learned from their Father in heaven. Our God is no fair-weather Father. He's not into this love-'em-and-leave-'em stuff. I can count on him to be in my corner no matter how I perform. You can, too.

The Great House of God

STOP

*You'll give up on yourself
before God will.*

Bury God's Name in Your Heart

When you are confused about the future, go to your *Jehovah-raah*, your caring shepherd. When you are anxious about provision, talk to *Jehovah-jireh*, the Lord who provides. Are your challenges too great? Seek the help of *Jehovah-shalom*, the Lord is peace. Is your body sick? Are your emotions weak? *Jehovah-rophe*, the Lord who heals you, will see you now. Do you feel like a soldier stranded behind enemy lines? Take refuge in *Jehovah-nissi*, the Lord my banner.

Meditating on the names of God reminds you of the character of God. Take these names and bury them in your heart.

God is

    the shepherd who guides,

        the Lord who provides,

            the voice who brings peace in the storm,

            the physician who heals the sick, and

            the banner that guides the soldier.

        And most of all, he . . . is.

          The Great House of God

STOP

If your God is mighty enough to ignite the sun, could it be that he is mighty enough to light your path?

God Is Cheering for You

God is for you. Not "maybe," not "has been," not "was," not "would be," but "God is!" He is for you. Today. At this hour. At this minute. As you read this sentence. No need to wait in line or come back tomorrow. He is with you. He could not be closer than he is at this second. His loyalty won't increase if you are better nor lessen if you are worse. He is for you.

God is *for you.* Turn to the sidelines; that's God cheering your run. Look past the finish line; that's God applauding your steps. Listen for him in the bleachers, shouting your name. Too tired to continue? He'll carry you. Too discouraged to fight? He's picking you up. God is *for* you.

God is for *you.* Had he a calendar, your birthday would be circled. If he drove a car, your name would be on his bumper. If there's a tree in heaven, he's carved your name in the bark. We know he has a tattoo, and we knows what it says. "I have written your name on my hand," he declares (Isa. 49:16).

In the Grip of Grace

STOP

My eternal soul is under heavenly coverage, and Jesus isn't known for dismissing clients.

What We Really Want to Know

Here is what we want to know. We want to know how long God's love will endure. . . . Not just on Easter Sunday when our shoes are shined and our hair is fixed. We want to know (deep within, don't we really want to know?), how does God feel about me when I'm a jerk? Not when I'm peppy and positive and ready to tackle world hunger. Not then. I know how he feels about me then. Even I like me then.

I want to know how he feels about me when I snap at anything that moves, when my thoughts are gutter-level, when my tongue is sharp enough to slice a rock. How does he feel about me then? . . .

That's what we want to know. . . .

Untethered by time, he sees us all. From the backwoods of Virginia to the business district of London. . . . Vagabonds and ragamuffins all, he saw us before we were born.

And he loves what he sees. Flooded by emotion. Overcome by pride, the Starmaker turns to us, one by one, and says, "You are my child. I love you dearly. I'm aware that someday you'll turn from me and walk away. But I want you to know, I've already provided you a way back."

In the Grip of Grace

*When Jesus went home,
he left the front door open.*

A Home for Your Heart

Chances are you've given little thought to housing your soul. We create elaborate houses for our bodies, but our souls are relegated to a hillside shanty where the night winds chill us and the rain soaks us. Is it any wonder the world is so full of cold hearts?

Doesn't have to be this way. We don't have to live outside. It's not God's plan for your heart to roam as a Bedouin. God wants you to move in out of the cold and live . . . with him. Under his roof there is space available. At his table a plate is set. In his living room a wingback chair is reserved just for you. And he'd like you to take up residence in his house. Why would he want you to share his home?

Simple, he's your Father.

The Great House of God

STOP

If God cares enough about the planet Saturn to give it rings or Venus to make it sparkle, is there an outside chance that he cares enough about you to meet your needs?

He Did It for You

Why did God do it? A shack would have sufficed, but he gave us a mansion. Did he have to give the birds a song and the mountains a peak? Was he required to put stripes on the zebra and the hump on the camel? Would we have known the difference had he made the sunsets gray instead of orange? . . . Why wrap creation in such splendor? Why go to such trouble to give such gifts?

Why do you? You do the same. I've seen you searching for a gift. I've seen you stalking the malls and walking the aisles. I'm not talking about the obligatory gifts. I'm not describing the last-minute purchase of drugstore perfume on the way to the birthday party. Forget blue-light specials and discount purchases; I'm talking about that extra-special person and that extra-special gift. . . . Why do you do it? You do it so the eyes will pop. You do it so the heart will stop. You do it to hear those words of disbelief, "You did this for *me*?"

That's why you do it. And that is why God did it. Next time a sunrise steals your breath or a meadow of flowers leaves you speechless, remain that way. Say nothing and listen as heaven whispers, "Do you like it? I did it just for you."

The Great House of God

*What is impossible with man
is possible with God
(Matt. 19:26).*

What Size Is God?

Nature is God's workshop. The sky is his resume. The universe is his calling card. You want to know who God is? See what he has done. You want to know his power? Take a look at his creation. Curious about his strength? Pay a visit to his home address: 1 Billion Starry Sky Avenue. . . .

He is untainted by the atmosphere of sin,
  unbridled by the time line of history,
    unhindered by the weariness of the body.

What controls you doesn't control him. What troubles you doesn't trouble him. What fatigues you doesn't fatigue him. Is an eagle disturbed by traffic? No, he rises above it. Is the whale perturbed by a hurricane? Of course not, he plunges beneath it. Is the lion flustered by the mouse standing directly in his way? No, he steps over it.

How much more is God able to soar above, plunge beneath, and step over the troubles of the earth!

The Great House of God

The cost of your sins is more than you can pay. The gift of your God is more than you can imagine.

God Is Your Home

Don't think you are separated from God, he at the top end of a great ladder, you at the other. Dismiss any thought that God is on Venus while you are on earth. Since God is Spirit (John 4:23), he is next to you: God himself is our roof. God himself is our wall. And God himself is our foundation.

Moses knew this. "Lord," he prayed, "you have been our home since the beginning" (Ps. 90:1). What a powerful thought: God as your home. Your home is the place where you can kick off your shoes and eat pickles and crackers and not worry about what people think when they see you in your bathrobe.

Your home is familiar to you. No one has to tell you how to locate your bedroom; you don't need directions to the kitchen. After a hard day scrambling to find your way around in the world, it's assuring to come home to a place you know. God can be equally familiar to you. With time you can learn where to go for nourishment, where to hide for protection, where to turn for guidance. Just as your earthly house is a place of refuge, so God's house is a place of peace. God's house has never been plundered, his walls have never been breached.

The Great House of God

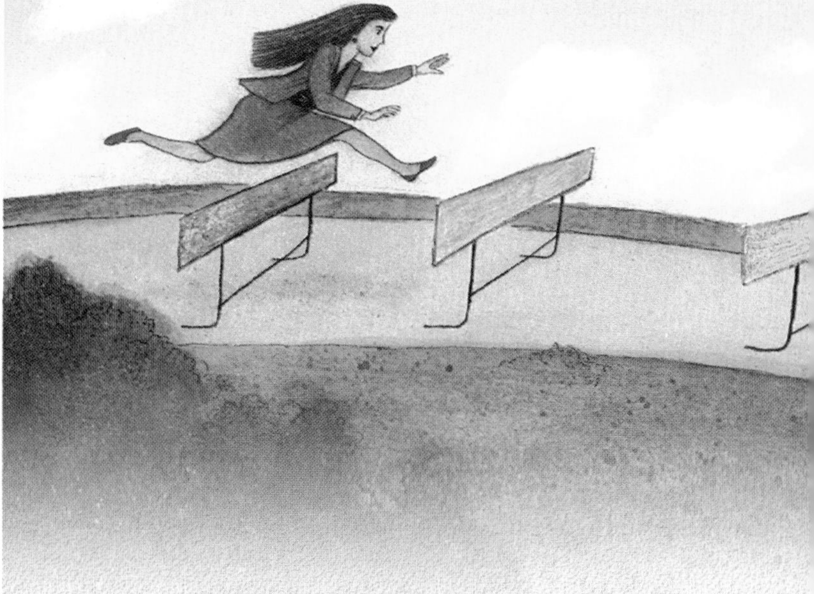

STOP

In the chapel of worship—we take our mind off ourselves and set it on God. The emphasis is on him.

Put a Bounce in Your Step

Some years ago a sociologist accompanied a group of mountain climbers on an expedition. Among other things, he observed a distinct correlation between cloud cover and contentment. When there was no cloud cover and the peak was in view, the climbers were energetic and cooperative. When the gray clouds eclipsed the view of the mountaintop, though, the climbers were sullen and selfish.

The same thing happens to us. As long as our eyes are on God's majesty there is a bounce in our step. But let our eyes focus on the dirt beneath us and we will grumble about every rock and crevice we have to cross. For this reason Paul urged, "Don't shuffle along, eyes to the ground, absorbed with the things right in front of you. Look up, and be alert to the things going on around Christ—that's where the action is. See things from his perspective" (Col. 3:1–2 MSG).

The Great House of God

*Faith in the future begets
power in the present.*

God's Thoughts

WE ASK FOR GRACE, ONLY TO FIND
FORGIVENESS ALREADY OFFERED.
(HOW DID YOU KNOW I WOULD SIN?)

We ask for food, only to find provision already made. (How did you know I would be hungry?)

We ask for guidance, only to find answers in God's ancient story. (How did you know what I would ask?)

God dwells in a different realm. . . .

God's thoughts are not our thoughts, nor are they even *like* ours. We aren't even in the same neighborhood. We're thinking, *Preserve the body*; he's thinking, *Save the soul.* We dream of a pay raise. He dreams of raising the dead. We avoid pain and seek peace. God uses pain to bring peace. "I'm going to live before I die," we resolve. "Die, so you can live," he instructs. We love what rusts. He loves what endures. We rejoice at our successes. He rejoices at our confessions. We show our children the Nike star with the million-dollar smile and say, "Be like Mike." God points to the crucified carpenter with bloody lips and a torn side and says, "Be like Christ."

The Great House of God

Teach Us to Pray

OUR FATHER
THANK YOU FOR ADOPTING ME
INTO YOUR FAMILY.

who is
Thank you, my Lord,
for being a God of the present tense:
my Jehovah-jireh (the God who provides),
my Jehovah-raah (the caring Shepherd),
my Jehovah-shalom (the Lord is peace),
my Jehovah-rophe (the God who heals),
and my Jehovah-nissi (Lord, my banner).

in heaven,
Your workshop of creation reminds me: If you can make
the skies, you can make sense out of my struggles.

Hallowed be thy name.
Be holy in my heart.
You are a "cut above" all else.
Enable me to set my sights on you.

Thy kingdom come,
Come kingdom!
Be present, Lord Jesus!
Have free reign in every corner of my life.

Thy will be done,
Reveal your heart to me, dear Father.
Show me my role in your passion.

On earth as it is in heaven.
Thank you that you silence heaven to hear my prayer.

Give us this day our daily bread.
I accept your portion for my life today.
I surrender my concerns regarding my well-being.

Forgive us our debts,
I thank you for the roof of grace over my head,
bound together with the timbers and nails of Calvary.
There is nothing I can do to earn or add to your mercy.
I confess my sins to you.

As we also have forgiven our debtors;
Treat me, Father, as I treat others.

Lead us not into temptation,
Let my small hand be engulfed in yours.
Hold me lest I fall.

Our Father. . . give us . . . forgive us . . . lead us
Let your kindness be on all your church.
I pray especially for ministers near
and missionaries far away.

Thine—not mine—is *the kingdom,*
I lay my plans at your feet.

Thine—not mine—is *the power,*
I come to you for strength.

Thine—not mine—is *the glory,*
I give you all the credit.

Forever. Amen.

The Great House of God

My personal goals

three-month goals _____
_____
_____
_____

six-month goals _____
_____
_____
_____

one-year goals _____
_____
_____
_____

two-year goals _____
_____
_____
_____

four-year goals _____
_____
_____
_____

lifetime goals _____
_____
_____
_____

Steps I have taken to reach my goals:

three-month goals _____

_____

_____

six-month goals _____

_____

_____

one-year goals _____

_____

_____

two-year goals _____

_____

_____

four-year goals _____

_____

_____

lifetime goals _____

_____

_____

Favorite verses of Scripture, quotes, poems, sayings:

Favorite books and songs:

_____
_____
_____
_____
_____
_____
_____
_____
_____
_____
_____
_____
_____
_____
_____
_____
_____
_____
_____

Places to see.
Things to do.

Saw it!
Did it!

Notes

Notes

Notes